COL & PHILEMON

A SELF-STUDY GUIDE

Irving L. Jensen

MOODY PRESS
CHICAGO

©1973 by
THE MOODY BIBLE INSTITUTE
OF CHICAGO

ISBN: 0-8024-4469-5

1 2 3 4 5 6 7 Printing/EP/Year 94 93 92 91 90

Printed in the United States of America

Contents

Introduction

The apostle Paul did some of his best thinking and writing as he sat chained for months in a Roman prison. From this time of confinement his remarkable prison epistles have come to us. They are remarkable for their wealth of content and conciseness of expression.

While in prison, Paul received an unexpected visitor, the slave of his old friend Philemon. After a mutually rewarding visit, Paul sent Onesimus back to Philemon with Tychicus, another of Paul's friends, and two letters, one for all the Christians of Colosse and one for Philemon personally.

The contents of these two short letters have contributed immeasurably to our understanding of proper doctrine and Christian living. If you study them carefully, Colossians and Philemon will prove effective in your life as they were to the original readers. And may you, as one whom Paul addressed, learn that "in all things he [Christ] might have the preeminence."

Suggestions for Study

1. Spend most of your Bible study time studying the words and phrases of the Bible text itself. God inspired it and made it profitable for everyone, not just for men and women trained in Hebrew and Greek. This study guide is to be used in addition to, not instead of, your own study of the Bible.

2. Use a special Bible for study. Get one with large print and wide margins, and write in it freely. One good idea is to mark where each new paragraph begins as you study Colossians and Philemon. Underline words and phrases that strike you, and write out the answers in this manual. Record as many thoughts and answers as you can on the analytical charts provided.

3. Your own time of meditation is an important phase in Bible study. What did the text mean to those who first received it? What does it mean to you?

Study Steps

Most of the lessons in this book contain six main parts:

1. *Preparation for study.* These preliminary studies will help set the stage for your analysis by providing background and review to get you thinking in the right direction.

2. *Analysis.* This is the heart of all Bible study. Many questions are included in each lesson. Also worksheets (e.g., analytical charts) for recording observations and survey charts for views of context appear throughout the manual.

3. *Notes.* The comments made here are usually about words and phrases whose meanings and background are not fully given by the immediate context.

4. *For thought and discussion.* This part of the lesson stresses application of the Bible text and will be of special interest if you are studying in a group.

5. *Further study.* Related subjects for extended study are identified here. Continuity in the lessons does not depend on your completing this phase.

6. *Words to ponder.* The concluding note is offered to encourage you to reflect upon the Bible text you have just studied.

Suggestions to Group Leaders

1. Determine how much of each lesson may be adequately studied at each group meeting. Assign homework accordingly. Remind your group to write out answers to all questions.

2. Start the meeting on time and close on time. Extended discussions and counseling may continue after the group session is officially closed.

3. Stimulate discussion during the class meeting. Encourage everyone to participate by asking questions, answering questions, sharing views, and giving testimonies.

4. If possible, reproduce on chalkboard or poster paper the major charts and diagrams of the manual. An overhead projector is especially valuable for this. Discussions can be kept from aimless wandering by periodic reference to the context represented in chart form in full view of everyone.

5. Help the members choose the right kinds of extra aids for Bible study. (A list of books for further help is at the back of this manual.) Here are five basic sources: a Bible dictionary or encyclopedia, a modern version (such as the *New American Standard Bible*), a modern paraphrase (such as *The Living Bible*), an exhaustive concordance, a commentary, and a book on word studies.

6. Devote the last part of your meeting to sharing the spiritual lessons taught by the Bible passage. This should be the climax of the group session.

7. You are the key to the atmosphere of the class. Aim to keep it relaxed, frank, sincere, interesting, and challenging.

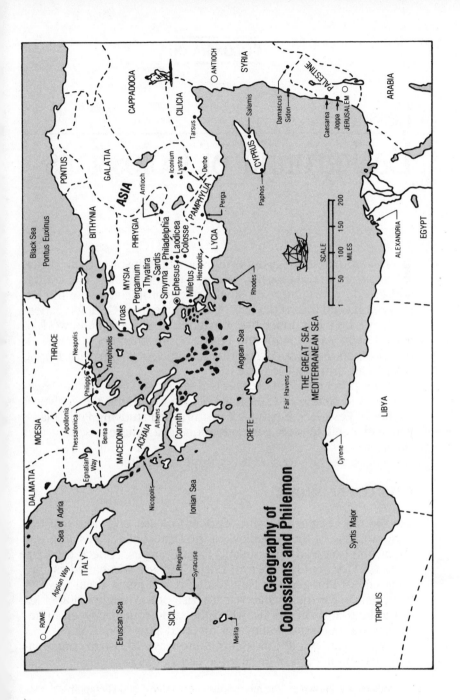

Geography of Colossians and Philemon

7

Lesson 1
Background of Colossians

In this study, we are considering one of the inspiring letters that Paul wrote in prison—the epistle to the Colossians. The church addressed by this letter was small and inconspicuous, but the letter itself had all the credentials of a message from God. Its readers could not help but notice that it magnifies the Person and work of Jesus Christ. As we study the epistle's four chapters, let us seek new insights into the riches of intimate fellowship with Christ, who "is all, and in all" (3: 11).

The purpose of this lesson is to acquaint you with the background and setting of Colossians before beginning the analytical studies in Lesson 3. If you have just finished studying Philippians, you will need to shift your attention to a different setting and situation.

(Note: be sure to read every Bible verse cited.)

I. THE CITY OF COLOSSE

See the map of the area surrounding Colosse, and note that Colosse was one of the "tri-cities" of the Lycus Valley. This area was about one hundred miles inland from Ephesus. (Check the map on p. 6.) Five centuries before Christ, Colosse was hailed as "the great city of Phrygia." By Paul's time, it was just a small town. A main reason for the change was the rise of the neighboring cities of Laodicea and Hierapolis, when the trade route between Ephesus and the Euphrates Valley was diverted away from Colosse.[1]

When Paul wrote Colossians, there was a Christian congregation meeting in each of these three cities (4:13).

1. Laodicea was known as "the metropolis of the valley," and Hierapolis, "the sacred city."

ENVIRONS OF COLOSSE

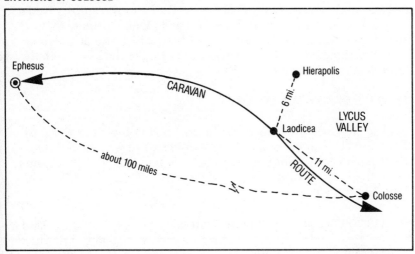

The inhabitants of Colosse were mainly Greeks and Phrygians, along with an unusually large Jewish population. The area was famous for its soft wool.

II. THE CHURCH AT COLOSSE

Paul's evangelistic and teaching ministry at Ephesus on his third missionary journey may have had much to do with the founding of the church at Colosse.[2] From Colossians 1:3-4 (cf. 2:1) some conclude that the congregation for the most part were strangers to Paul. Epaphras, who may have been one of Paul's Ephesian converts, could have been the founder of this church (1:7) as well as of the churches of Laodicea and Hierapolis (cf. 4:13). At any rate he was a key member of the Colossian congregation (4:12).

Colossians 4:17 suggests that Archippus may have been the church's pastor when Paul wrote the epistle. (Cf. Philem. 2.) The church assembled in the home of Philemon, who was one of its active members (4:9; Philem. 1, 5-7). How large the group was, we do not know. Most of the members were of Greek background. The others were converted Jews.

2. The journey (A.D.52-55) is recorded in Acts 18:23–21:17. Read especially 19:10, 26.

III. AUTHOR AND DESTINATION OF THE EPISTLE

Colossians 1:1 identifies the author as Paul and recognizes Paul's co-worker Timothy in its greeting. Verse 2 identifies the readers as "the saints and faithful brethren in Christ which are at Colosse." Paul also directed the Colossian church to share the letter with the church at Laodicea (4:16; cf. 2:1).

IV. PLACE OF WRITING AND DATE

Paul wrote wrote this epistle from prison at Rome, around A.D.61. His letters to Philemon and the Ephesians were written and delivered at the same time. (See Chart A.) Tychicus and Onesimus were the bearers of the letters. (See Eph. 6:21-22; Col 4:7-9; Philem. 12, 23-24.)

CHRONOLOGICAL ORDER OF THE PAULINE EPISTLES   **Chart A**

MISSIONARY TOURS	FIRST IMPRISONMENT	RELEASE	FINAL IMPRISONMENT
A.D. 48-56	61-62	62-67	67
GALATIANS— between tours 1 and 2 ------- tour 1 THESSALONIANS ⌉ ⊢2 2 THESSALONIANS ⌋ ------- tour 1 CORINTHIANS ⌉ 2 CORINTHIANS ⊢3 ROMANS ⌋	COLOSSIANS PHILEMON EPHESIANS --------- PHILIPPIANS	1 TIMOTHY --------- TITUS	2 TIMOTHY
6 EPISTLES	4 EPISTLES	2 EPISTLES	1 EPISTLE

V. OCCASION FOR WRITING

The immediate occasion for writing this letter was heresy in the church at Colosse. (The pronunciation of the two words together, Colosse-Heresy is a help in recalling the setting of this epistle.) Epaphras reported to Paul the false views and evil practices in the church at that time. (Cf. 1: 7-8.) The section 2:8-23 describes these rather explicitly, though Paul does not name or identify the heresy itself. It would probably be more accurate to use the plural word *heresies*, for a variety of false views were being fostered by the false teachers. Among these were: (1) a Judaistic legalism—circumcision (2:11; 3:11), ordinances (2:14), foods, holidays, et cetera (2:16); (2) a severe asceticism (2:16, 20-23); (3) worship of angels (2:18); and (4) glorification and worship of human knowledge (2:8).

These false views will be discussed in more detail in a later lesson. The important observation we make here is that Paul ably challenged and exploded these heresies on a positive note, by a pure presentation of counter-truths about the Person and work of Jesus Christ. (Read Philem. 23 to learn what may have befallen Epaphras after delivering his report to Paul.)

VI. THEME AND TONE

The main theme of Colossians is well represented by the text "Christ is all, and in all" (3:11). As someone has said, "Paul does not preach a system nor a philosophy but a person—Jesus Christ." The deity of Christ, the efficacy of His death on the cross, His sovereignty and supreme lordship, and His continuing mediatorship are all part of Paul's doctrinal message, because these were the doctrines being denied by the false teachers. Other important subjects appearing in the epistle will be observed in our survey study.

The tone throughout the epistle is forthright, positive, bold. Paul takes the offensive, not defensive, position. He has his sword at his side as he writes to the Christians at Colosse. He would agree wholeheartedly with the comment that "the only safeguard against a false intellectual system is a strong and positive Christian theology." But there is a tone of compassion in the epistle as well. As one writer has remarked, "it breathes the spirit of tenderest love and joy in all sorrows and afflictions."

VII. RELATION TO OTHER NEW TESTAMENT BOOKS

Colossians is one of the four prison epistles, the other three being Ephesians, Philippians, and Philemon. All four were written about the same time (A.D. 61-62), which would account for at least some of the similarities in the books.

Colossians and Ephesians have been called twin epistles because of their many likenesses. Both were written with the same general purpose—to show the relationship between Christ and

11

His church, as assurance and correction to young Christians maturing in the Lord. But the two epistles are far from being identical twins. Study Chart B to learn some of the differences.

The place of Colossians in the foursome of Romans, Galatians, Ephesians, and Colossians may also be noted.

COLOSSIANS AND EPHESIANS COMPARED   **Chart B**

COLOSSIANS	EPHESIANS
Christ and the cosmos	Christ and the church
emphasis on Christ, Head of the church	emphasis on the church, Body of Christ
more personal; local	less personal; lofty
combats error directly	combats error indirectly
tone: intensity and tumult of a battlefield	tone: calmness of surveying the field after victory

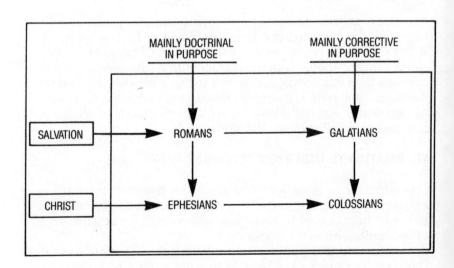

12

Review Questions

1. How large a city was Colosse in the days of Paul?

How far was it from Ephesus?

2. Did Paul have anything to do with the founding of the church at Colosse? If so, what?

3. Name some active members of the congregation.

Who may have been the pastor when Paul wrote Colossians?

4. Was Paul acquainted with most of the congregation by sight?

5. Where were the two nearest churches located?

6. Where was Paul when he wrote Colossians, and when did he write?

7. What was the immediate occasion for writing this letter?

8. What serious problems threatened the Colossian church?

9. What approach did Paul use in writing to the church?

10. Who else besides the Colossians did Paul want to read the letter?

_____

_____

11. What is the main theme of Colossians?

_____

_____

12. Compare the theme and purpose of Colossians with each of the following: Ephesians, Galatians, Romans.

_____

_____

_____

_____

_____

_____

_____

_____

_____

THE PLACE OF THE CHRISTOLOGICAL EPISTLES IN THE NEW TESTAMENT

NEW TESTAMENT

HISTORY	EPISTLES					APOCALYPSE
	Pauline				General	
	EARLY	LATER				
	during missionary journeys	after arrest at Jerusalem				
		FIRST IMPRISONMENT ("prison epistles")	RELEASE	SECOND IMPRISONMENT		
		CHRISTOLOGICAL	PASTORAL			
MATTHEW					JAMES	REVELATION
MARK	GALATIANS	COLOSSIANS	1 TIMOTHY		HEBREWS	
LUKE	1 THESSALONIANS	EPHESIANS	TITUS		JUDE	
JOHN	2 THESSALONIANS	PHILEMON			1 PETER	
ACTS	1 CORINTHIANS	PHILIPPIANS		2 TIMOTHY	2 PETER	
	2 CORINTHIANS				1 JOHN	
	ROMANS				2 JOHN	
					3 JOHN	

Lesson 2
Survey of Colossians

In this lesson we begin a study of the actual text of Colossians, observing the epistle's general structure and content. This is what is called survey study. Survey should always come before analysis. This standard procedure is expressed by the maxim "Image the whole, then execute the parts."

The directions given below will guide your survey study. Do not tarry over details, but keep scanning, ever moving, discovering new features of the panorama as you go along.

I. A FIRST SCANNING

Scan the entire epistle in one sitting. List your general impressions.

II. PARAGRAPH TITLES

Secure paragraph titles for each paragraph. Record your titles on Chart C. (Two examples are given.)

PARAGRAPH TITLES OF COLOSSIANS Chart C

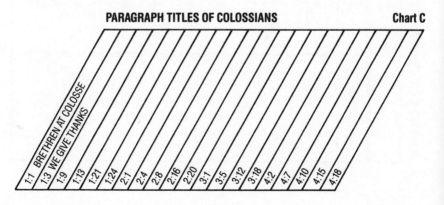

COLOSSIANS: CHRIST IS ALL AND IN ALL

KEY VERSE: 3:11b

KEY WORDS: mystery, knowledge, wisdom, fulness, perfect, all (16 times in chap. 1), faith, body, love, prayer

MAINLY PERSONAL

OPENING BENEDICTION

1:1

1:3 We give thanks

We pray

Explanation of the Person and work of Christ

1:13

MAINLY DOCTRINAL

2:4 Exposing of heresies
1. legalism (Judaistic) 2:11-17
2. worship of human mind 2:8
3. angel worship 2:18
4. asceticism 2:20-23

3:5 Exchanges in Christian's conduct
PUT OFF/PUT ON
1. in personal life 3:5-17
2. in domestic life 3:18—4:1
3. in relation to the world 4:2-6

MAINLY PRACTICAL

4:7 NOTES AND SALUTATIONS
fellow bond slave 4:7
fellow prisoner 4:10
fellow worker 4:11

4:18b CLOSING BENEDICTION

MAINLY PERSONAL

Tone	personal	doctrinal	polemical	hortatory	personal
Theme	CHRIST YOUR INHERITANCE 1:12	CHRIST YOUR INDWELLER 1:27	CHRIST YOUR SUFFICIENCY 2:10	CHRIST YOUR MOTIVATION 3:17	CHRIST YOUR MASTER 4:7
Topic	true doctrine		false doctrine	Christian living	Christian fellowship

17

III. SUBSEQUENT READINGS

Read through the epistle a few more times, looking for:
  (a) Organization of content (e.g., introduction, main body, conclusion)
  (b) Types of content (e.g., doctrine, practice)
  (c) Key words and phrases
  (d) A prominent theme

IV. SURVEY CHART

Chart D is a completed survey chart of Colossians. After you have looked it over at least in a general way, follow the study suggestions given. Time well spent here will be generously rewarded in the analytical studies that follow.

1. Note on the chart the opening and closing benedictions. Also note the two sections identified as "Personal." Read the Bible passages involved, to justify these descriptions. The section called "Mainly Doctrinal" begins at 1:13 because a major concentration on the subject of Christ is introduced here ("his dear Son"), to be developed in the verses that follow.

In the survey studies suggested below you will want to find out why major divisions on Chart D are also made at 2:4, 3:5, and 4:7.

2. Note the three parts of the main body of the epistle. Polemical means that which refutes errors of doctrine. Hortatory as used here includes both exhortation and command.

3. Read 2:4, and observe how in this verse Paul begins to write about false teachers threatening the Christians at Colosse. Read also the opening phrases of 2:8, 16, 18.

4. Note on the chart that the hortatory section begins at 3:5. Read paragraph 3:1-4. You will observe that this paragraph is also of a hortatory nature. But it is included in the previous section ("Polemical," 2:4-3:4) because it is closely related to paragraph 2:20-23. (For example, compare the first phrases of 2:20 and 3:1).

5. The concluding personal section begins at 4:7, because here Paul begins to bring in personal notes and salutations.

6. Colossians is basically of three types of writings: doctrinal, practical, and personal. Note the outline at the top of the chart showing this.

7. Study the other outlines that represent the content of the major divisions of Colossians.

8. Note the title chosen for the book; also the key verse and key words.

V. CONCLUDING EXERCISES

Before leaving this overview phase of study, read through the entire epistle, noting the times Christ is mentioned (either as Christ or by other names and titles). Make a list showing what Paul writes about Christ in each instance. This study will support the conclusion that the fundamental thought of Colossians is Christ, the Head of all things.

Review Questions

1. What are the different types of content in the epistle to the Colossians?

_____

_____

Can you recall the outline, showing where each new section begins?
2. Does Paul here follow his usual pattern of writing about doctrine as a foundation, before giving appeals for Christian living?

_____

_____

3. What title is assigned to Colossians on the chart?

_____

4. Try to complete this outline:

Christ Your Inheritance; _____;

_____; _____; _____.
5. How any key words shown on Chart D can you recall?

_____

_____

_____

_____

_____

_____

_____

_____

Lesson 3

Thanksgiving and Intercession

The first passage for our detailed analysis of Colossians is the opening personal section of twelve verses. The letter begins on a bright note, typical of Paul's writings. There is no clue here that a heavy burden concerning problems at Colosse lay on the apostle's heart, yet that was the reason for the letter.

I. PREPARATION FOR STUDY

Write a list of good traits that you think a local Christian church should exemplify. After you have completed your study of 1:1-12, go back to this list and see how the Colossian church rated.

II. AN ANALYSIS

Segments to be analyzed: 1:1-2 and 1:3-12
Paragraph divisions: at verses 1, 3, 9

A. General Analysis

1. Mark the paragraph divisions in your Bible.
2. Read the two segments through once for general impressions. In the King James Version how many sentences compose the second paragraph? the third paragraph? This style of translation reflects Paul's thinking: each phrase bringing on the next, and very intimately related to it.[1]

---

1. Modern versions usually translate the Greek text into shorter sentences, for easier reading. Actually, the original autographs did not contain punctuation marks.

What is the core (main subject, verb, object) of the second paragraph?

_____

_____

What is the core of the third paragraph?

_____

_____

_____

How do the two paragraphs differ from each other, as to main theme?

_____

_____

B. Paragraph Analysis

1. *Paragraph 1:1-2: Salutation*
Compare this salutation with that of Philippians. Compare it also with those of the other two prison epistles, Ephesians and Philemon. What is suggested by each of the following designations:

apostle of Jesus Christ

_____

apostle by the will of God

_____

our brother

_____

saints

_____

faithful brethren

_____

in Christ

_____

2. *Paragraph 1:3-8· We give thanks*
A good way to begin an analysis of this paragraph is to re-create the text, phrase by phrase. Read the text in your Bible carefully as you complete the following textual re-creation:

"WE GIVE THANKS _____

    praying _____

    since _____ of _____

                        and of _____

FOR THE HOPE which _____

    whereof _____ gospel;

      which _____

         as _____

        and _____

         as _____

        since _____

         and _____

    as ye also learned from Epaphras

          _____

        who _____

        who _____ ."

For what did Paul give thanks?

_____

What do verses 4 and 8 suggest as to the extent of Paul's acquaintance with the Colossians?

_____

_____

What did Paul mean by "in all the world" (1:6)?

_____

_____

3. *Paragraph 1:9-12: "We pray for you"*
Let us do a textual re-creation of this paragraph as well.

"
_____

WE ALSO   since _____

DO NOT CEASE to PRAY FOR YOU, and to DESIRE

that _____

     in _____ ;

that _____ ,

     being, _____ ,

and increasing _____ ;

     strengthened, _____ ,

        according to, _____ ,

        unto _____

        with _____ ;

giving _____ Father,

which (who) _____
_____ . ''

What is the main core of this long sentence?

_____

_____

What did Paul pray on behalf of the Christians at Colosse?

_____

_____

_____

How are the following related to each other in the Christian's life, according to this passage: knowledge of God, fruitfulness, power, thanksgiving?

_____

_____

_____

_____

_____

Note the repetition of similar terms in 1:11: *strengthened, might, power.*
Compare inheritance (1:12) and hope (1:5).

III. NOTES

1. *"For you a faithful minister of Christ"* (1:7). *The Living Bible* paraphrase of this phrase is, "He is Jesus Christ's slave, here in your place to help us." The phrase "for you" (KJV*) reads "on our behalf" in the NASB† and other versions based on earlier manuscripts. If the latter phrase is the reading of the original, it suggests that Epaphras pastored the church at Colosse as an understudy of Paul, similar to the way that Timothy ministered at Ephesus, and Titus at Crete.

2. *"Filled with the knowledge of his will"* (1:9). One of the heresies being advanced at the Colossian church was an incipient form of gnosticism, which among other things glorified human wisdom. Did Paul have this in mind when he wrote about "the knowledge of his will"? E. Earle Ellis writes, "There is probably a subtle contrast here with the knowledge *(gnosis)* of the Gnosticizing advocates: Paul emphasizes neither an abstract intellectualism nor an occult experience of the "powers," but a thorough knowledge *(epignosis)* of God's will in accordance with wisdom . . . and perception."[2]

3. *"Made us meet to be partakers of"* (1:12). The NASB reads, "Qualified us to share in."

IV. FOR THOUGHT AND DISCUSSION

1. Read this passage in a modern paraphrase. If you are studying in a group you will find it stimulating to discuss the practical spiritual truths taught here.
2. Here are some specific subjects to think about:
   (a) The intercession of Christians for their brothers in Christ
   (b) What it means to have a "hope laid up in heaven"
   (c) How faith, hope, and love are related to each other in Christian living (see vv. 4-5)

---

*King James Version.
†*New American Standard Bible.*
2. E. Earle Ellis, "The Epistle to the Colossians," p. 1337.

(d) How the gospel can bring forth fruit daily in a Christian's life
(e) What it means to have "spiritual understanding" (1:9)
(f) The richness of a joy that rises out of suffering (1:11)

V. FURTHER STUDY

Study the word *apostle* as it is used in the New Testament. Consider such areas as the apostle's authorization, mission, and responsibility.

VI. WORDS TO PONDER

Epaphras . . . a faithful minister of Christ (Col. 1:7). Well done, thou good and faithful servant (Matt. 25:21).

Lesson 4

Colossians 1:13–2:3

The Person and
Work of Christ

Paul has one thing in mind as he writes the next lines of his letter—to exalt Jesus as God and Savior. There is a specific reason
for this. One of the heresies at Colosse was the worship of angels,
with its denial of Christ's deity. Before Paul exposes such heresies
specifically (2:4–3:4), he chooses first to proclaim the positive
counter-truths about the Person and work of Christ. This is the
subject of this lesson. The passage itself is the major doctrinal section of the epistle.

I. PREPARATION FOR STUDY

1. Have a mental picture of where this passage is in the context of the entire epistle. Chart E shows the relationships.

CONTEXT OF COLOSSIANS 1:13—2:3   **Chart E**

Lesson 4

1:1	1:13	2:4	3:5	4:7 4:18
PERSONAL	DOCTRINAL	POLEMICAL	HORTATORY	PERSONAL
TRUE DOCTRINE		FALSE DOCTRINE	CHRISTIAN LIVING	CHRISTIAN FELLOWSHIP
	mainly doctrinal		mainly practical	mainly personal

2. Someone has said of Colossians, "Paul does not preach
here a system nor a philosophy, but a person—Jesus Christ."

26

Which is basic to the other: the doctrine of the *Person* of Christ or the doctrine of the *work* of Christ? Could Christ have done what He did if He was not who He was?

3. Read John 1: 1-18 for background of doctrines of Christ as taught in Colossians 1: 13-20.

II. ANALYSIS

Segment to be analyzed: 1:13–2:3
Paragraph divisions: at verses 1:13,[1] 21, 24; 2:1

A. General Analysis

1. After marking the paragraph divisions in your Bible, read through the segment once, for overall impressions.
2. Who is the prominent person of the passage? Who is the main person of each paragraph?

_____

_____

_____

Compare your answer with what is recorded in the narrow left-hand column of Chart F.
3. In which paragraphs does Paul write about his ministry for Christ?

_____

Compare your answer with the observation recorded on Chart F.
4. Which paragraph gives the fullest description of the Person and work of Christ? What is taught about Christ in each of the other paragraphs?
Record your observations on Chart F.

B. Paragraph Analysis

1. *Paragraph 1:13-20*
What is the main topic of this paragraph? (Note: as you study these verses, keep in mind that this is the key passage exposing the idolatry of worshiping angels.)

_____

_____

---

1. Even though 1:13 is not a new sentence in the KJV, we are studying it as the beginning of a new thought. The NASB begins verse 13 thus: "For He delivered us from..."

27

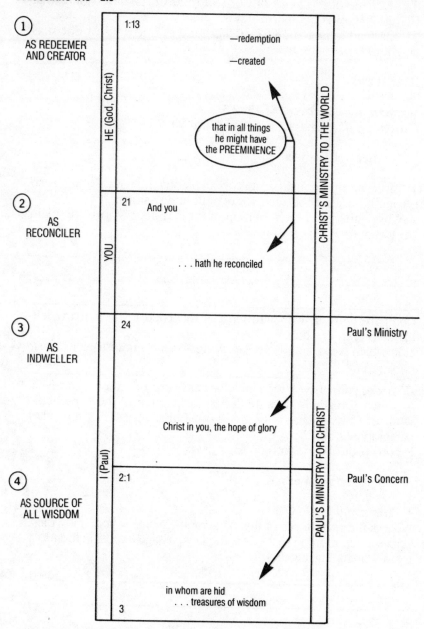

(1) AS REDEEMER AND CREATOR

(2) AS RECONCILER

(3) AS INDWELLER

(4) AS SOURCE OF ALL WISDOM

HE (God, Christ)

YOU

I (Paul)

1:13
—redemption
—created

that in all things he might have the PREEMINENCE

21 And you

. . . hath he reconciled

24

Christ in you, the hope of glory

2:1

in whom are hid . . . treasures of wisdom

3

CHRIST'S MINISTRY TO THE WORLD

PAUL'S MINISTRY FOR CHRIST

Paul's Ministry

Paul's Concern

Record below what is said in the paragraph about who Christ is (Person) and what He does (work).

PERSON OF CHRIST

_____   _____

_____   _____

_____   _____

_____   _____

WORK OF CHRIST

_____   _____

_____   _____

_____   _____

_____   _____

_____   _____

What are the references to Christ's death?

_____

_____

_____

_____

Read verse 13. What two realms are contrasted here?

_____

_____

How do the last three words introduce the verses that follow (verses 14-20)?

_____

_____

Read verse 14. What is meant by redemption?

_____

_____

What is the price of redemption? (Cf. 1 Pet. 1:18-19.)

_____

_____

What does forgiveness of sins have to do with redemption?

_____

How do the two phrases of 1:15 identify Christ?

_____

_____

Compare 2 Corinthians 4:6 and Hebrews 1:3.

_____

_____

Compare 1:16 with Genesis 1:1 and Hebrews 11:3.

_____

_____

_____

What does this reveal about who Jesus is?

_____

_____

What is the impact of the repeated phrase all things" in 1:16?

_____

_____

Are angels included as created beings?

_____

What two truths are taught by 1:17? (See Notes on the word *consist*.)

_____

_____

_____

On the basis of verses 18 and 19, how is Christ qualified to "have the preeminence"?

_____

_____

Read verse 20. What does "reconcile" mean? (Cf. 1:22.)

_____

Who initiates reconciliation?

_____

_____

How is this answered by the following progression:

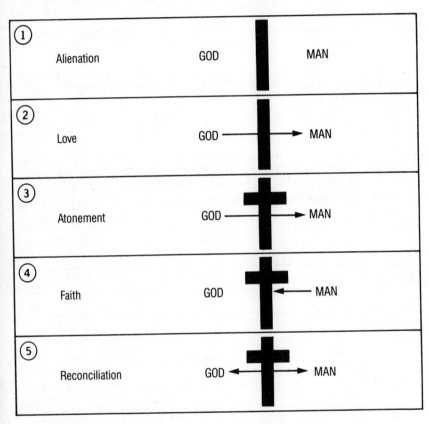

①	Alienation	GOD	MAN
②	Love	GOD ⟶	MAN
③	Atonement	GOD ⟶	MAN
④	Faith	GOD	⟵ MAN
⑤	Reconciliation	GOD ⟵	⟶ MAN

What is meant by each of these phrases of 1:20:
"by him"

_____

"all things"

_____

"unto himself"

_____

2. Paragraph 1:21-23

What is the ultimate purpose of reconciliation (1:22)?

_____

_____

What is the presentation of verse 22 conditioned upon (verse 23)?

_____

Is this "if" situation intended to take away assurance or to inspire watchfulness?

_____

What does the latter part of verse 23 teach about the gospel?

3. Paragraph 1:24-29

How does the last phrase of 1:23 introduce the theme of this paragraph?

_____

Compare two or three modern versions for their rendering of the phrase "fill up that which is behind of the afflictions of Christ" (1:24). Record what this paragraph teaches about Paul's ministry and his message:

Ministry

_____

_____

_____

_____

Message

_____

_____

_____

_____

What is the force of the phrase "in Christ Jesus" as it relates to "that we may present every man perfect?"

_____

Observe the five work terms in 1:29. What does this verse teach about Paul's ministry?

_____

_____

4. *Paragraph 2:1-3*
What was Paul's heart burden, according to this paragraph?

_____

_____

What different things did Paul wish for his Christian brethren?

_____

_____

Note the repetition of these similar terms in 2:2-3: *understanding; acknowledgment* (knowledge, NASB); *wisdom; knowledge.* Do you think Paul may have had the gnostic heresy in mind when he wrote these verses, since gnosticism glorifies human knowledge? What does he teach here about knowledge?

_____

_____

III. NOTES

1. *"Redemption through his blood"* (1:14). The price of redemption was nothing less than Jesus' blood. This is a primary reason for the Jews' rejection of Jesus as their Messiah. At a recent dialogue between Jewish and Christian scholars, Rabbi Samson H. Levey stated with conviction that "the doctrine of human blood for atonement of human sin—the Christian doctrine deriving from Jesus' crucifixion—would not be accepted by Jews."[2] Dr. Levey said that ever since Abraham was "not allowed" to sacrifice his son, the Jews have rejected the idea of human sacrifice.

2. *"Firstborn of every creature"* (1:15). Some interpret this phrase as "primeval Creator." On the word *firstborn* in this context, Kenneth Wuest writes:

2. Annual meeting of the Evangelical Theological Society, held at Westmont College, December 1970.

The Greek word implied two things, priority to all creation and sovereignty over all creation. In the first meaning we see the absolute pre-existence of the Logos. Since our Lord existed before all created things, He must be uncreated. Since He is uncreated, He is eternal. Since He is eternal, He is God. Since He is God, He cannot be one of the emanations from deity of which the Gnostic speaks. . . . [3]

3. *"By him all things consist"* (1:17). The NASB reads, "In Him all things hold together." Some have called this the Colossian Law, applying it to that unknown force that holds together the parts of each infinitesimal atomic universe. One scientist has written of this:

> You grasp what this implies. It implies that all the massive nuclei have no right to be alive at all. Indeed, they should never have been created, and, if created, they should have blown up instantly. Yet here they all are, and the rocks of the earth are full of these little high explosive clusters, all of them ready to separate. . . . And, yet, they never do sunder themselves. Some inflexible inhibition is holding them relentlessly together. The nature of the inhibition is also a secret, but here I suspect that it is neither a military secret nor a quantum-mechanical secret, but one thus far reserved by Nature for herself.[4]

4. *"All fulness"* (1: 19). This reference is the same as "all the fulness of the Godhead" in 2:9.

5. *"If ye continue"* (1:23). The warning of 1:23 is to prevent complacency. (Cf. 1 Cor. 9:27.) Ellis writes, "For the apostle, assurance always had to be present tense. And, while God's election is not vacillating, it can be affirmed only in terms of profession (cf. Ro 10:9), conduct (cf. 1 Co. 6:9), and the witness of the Spirit (cf. Ro. 8:9)"[5]

6. *"Love . . . knowledge"* (2:2). "Orthodoxy without love is sterile, and love apart from truth becomes 'mush;' but together they issue in spiritual apprehension, knowledge of the mystery of God."[6]

3. Kenneth S. Wuest, *Ephesians and Colossians in the Greek New Testament,* p. 183.
4. Karl K. Darrow, quoted by D. Lee Chesnut in *The Atom Speaks* (Grand Rapids: Eerdman, 1951), pp. 66-67.
5. E. Earle Ellis, "The Epistle to the Colossians," p. 1339.
6. Ibid., p. 1340.

IV. FOR THOUGHT AND DISCUSSION

1. What are your spiritual benefits, in view of who Christ is and what He has done? Be specific.

2. What spiritual lessons can be learned from Paul's example as a minister of Jesus Christ?

V. FURTHER STUDY

Two subjects recommended for extended study in the New Testament are:

(1) the Christian's identification with Christ in suffering. For example, compare 2 Corinthians 1:5-7; 4:12; 13:4; Philippians 3:10; 1 Peter 4:13; 5:9; Revelation 1:9.

(2) Christ as the firstborn. Compare these New Testament references: Romans 8:29; Colossians 1:15; Colossians 1:18; Hebrews 1:6; Revelation 1:5.

VI. WORDS TO PONDER

"His power, which mightily works within me," (Col. 1:29b, NASB).

Lesson 5

Heresies Exposed

Now Paul writes specifically about the heresies that threatened the life of the churches of the Lycus Valley. He does not name individuals or groups, but it is clear that he has false teachers in mind, from such phrases as "lest any man beguile you" (2:4); "lest any man spoil you" (2:8); "let no man . . . judge you" (2:16).

No Christian group—local church, school, other organization —is ever immune to Satan's subtle undermining through false teaching. Satan appears as an angel of light. He makes false teaching sound like true teaching to those whose minds he has first blinded. Paul knew how to diagnose such problems in the churches of Asia Minor and how to deal with them effectively. As you study this lesson, learn from the experience of the apostle so that you too will stand as a defender of the truth of the gospel.

I. PREPARATION FOR STUDY

1. Chart G shows what were probably the bases for the speculative doctrines of the Colossian heresy. Observe the following:

(a) The false religionists attempted to solve the problem of the great gulf. What was that problem?

(b) Two solutions were suggested:

(1) God reaching man by way of emanations from Himself, each successive emanation being of less holiness. How was Jesus regarded, as compared with angels?

(2) Man reaching God in the realm of mental activity. Why were mind and spirit worshiped?

(c) Since flesh was regarded as essentially evil, asceticism and legalism were the consequences. What is asceticism? Does the Bible teach that flesh *itself* is evil?

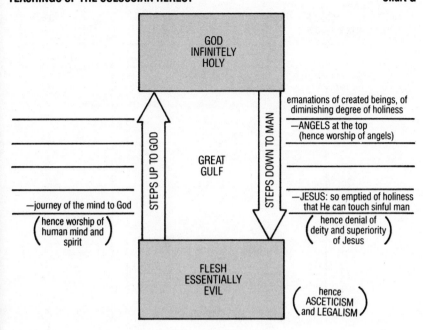

2. For the refreshment of your soul, read Colossians 2:1–3:4 in *The Living Bible*. This will be a warm introduction to your analytical studies of the text.

II. AN ANALYSIS

Segment to be analyzed: 2:4–3:4
Paragraph divisions: at verses 2:4, 8, 16, 20; 3:1. Mark these in your Bible.

A. General Analysis

1. Read the entire segment, noting Paul's references to false teachings. Compare the first verse of each of the first three paragraphs. Compare the first phrases of the last two paragraphs.
2. What verses refer directly or indirectly to each of the following: worship of angels

_____

denial of deity of Christ

_____

The Christian and
CHRIST

2:4	
	beguile you

8	
	spoil you

16	
	judge you

20	

3:1	

3:4	

speculation

---

deification of human knowledge

---

asceticism

Judaistic legalism

---

3. Look at each paragraph for references to the Christian's relation to Christ. Record this study in the right-hand margin of Chart H.
4. How does the last paragraph serve as a positive conclusion?

B. Paragraph Analysis

1. *Paragraph 2:4-7*
What is Paul's warning in verse 4?

How does Paul commend his readers in verse 5?

What is the simple yet vital command of verse 6?

In verses 6 and 7, Paul presents four bases which would enable the Colossians to fulfill the command of verse 6. What are they?
v.6*a*

---

v. 7

---

2. *Paragraph 2:8-15*
What is Paul's warning in verse 8?

What does Paul write about in the remainder of the paragraph?

_____

_____

Record below what is taught here about Christ and about the Christian.

CHRIST

_____

_____

_____

_____

_____

CHRISTIAN

_____

_____

_____

_____

_____

3. *Paragraph 2:16-19*
Use the following translations of the King James Version's phrases cited, to help clarify the meanings:
     2:17: "the body is Christ" (KJV)—"the reality is Christ" (TEV*)
     2:18: "in a voluntary humility" (KJV)—"delighting in self-abasement" (NASB)
What false teachings does Paul expose here?

_____

_____

In 2:17 what function does he assign to Old Testament laws?

_____

What are his denunciations of angel worship in 2:18-19?

_____

Today's English Version.

40

How is Christ exalted in 2:19?

_____

_____

4. *Paragraph 2:20-23*
What are Paul's criticisms of legalism and asceticism in these
verses?

_____

_____

In a practical way, what does it mean to be "dead with Christ"
(2:20)?

_____

_____

_____

5. *Paragraph 3:1-4*
What are the contrasts of this paragraph?

_____

_____

How does Paul derive motivation for everyday living from the believer's relation to Christ in the following:
Christ's death:

_____

Christ's resurrection:

_____

Christ's return:

_____

III. NOTES

1. *"Beguile"* (2:4). The Greek word so translated has the idea
of leading astray by fallacious reasoning.

2. *"Rudiments of the world"* (2:8). (See also 2:20.) The history
of the word translated "rudiments" accounts for two different interpretations made by commentators. "From 'things set in a row' it
came to mean the letters of the alphabet, then the rudiments of
any subject, and through various stages came to be applied to the
elements of the physical universe. Later it was used of the powers

believed to be controlling the universe."[1] The two different interpretations are (1) elemental dos and don'ts (see Galatians 4:9) and (2) angelic powers. Compare various versions and commentaries for their choices.

3. *"Putting off the body of the sins of the flesh"* (2:11). The "circumcision of Christ" referred to in this verse is a spiritual circumcision of the heart, in dealing with the old nature. Read Deuteronomy 30:6; Jeremiah 4:4; Romans 2:29; 6:6; Philippians 3:3.

4. *"Having spoiled"* (2:15). The word means stripped and was used of a captor who stripped his captives of most or all of their belongings, including clothing, to symbolize utter defeat.

5. *"Holyday...new moon...sabbath"* (2:16). These were annual, monthly, and weekly festivals, respectively.

6. *"The body is of Christ"* (2:17) "The substance belongs to Christ" (NASB); "the reality of Christ" (TEV); "the real thing... Christ Himself" (*The Living Bible*).

7. *"Dead with Christ"* (2:20). Ellis writes, "On Calvary the Christian died with Christ to the old age (the mortal Adamic race), and so he must not live as though the world (kosmos) or its ordinances still had a claim upon him (cf. Rom 6)."[2]

IV. FOR THOUGHT AND DISCUSSION

1. What does the word *philosophy* mean in general usage?[3] Consult a dictionary for definitions and examples. Is all philosophy based on false foundations? What does Paul mean by his reference in 2:8?

2. What are the limitations of human knowledge? Is man's reason sufficient to answer the great questions of life, such as, Where did I come from? Why am I here? and, Where am I going? What is the purpose of divine revelation?

3. Why is the doctrine of the deity of Christ vital in the Christian faith?

4. How can a sinner be restored to fellowship with God? Why is the observing of various rituals not sufficient for this?

5. What does it mean to you, in a practical way, to be "dead with Christ" (2:20) and also to be "risen with Christ" (3:1)?

1. J. Ithel Jones, "The Epistle to the Colossians," in *The New Bible Commentary*, p. 1048.
2. E. Earle Ellis, "The Epistle to the Colossians," p. 1342.
3. The English word *philosophy* is derived from *philo* (love) and *sophia* (wisdom).

V. FURTHER STUDY

Paul writes of the Colossians' steadfastness of faith (2:5). Read the following verses, and identify the degree or kind of faith referred to in each case:

Deut. 32:20; Mark 4:40

Matt. 8:26

Luke 7:9

Acts 11:24

Rom. 14: 1

---

1 Cor. 15:14

---

1 Tim. 1:5

James 2:5

James 2:17

---

2 Pet. 1:1

Jude 20

VI. WORDS TO PONDER

And now just as you trusted Christ to save you, trust Him too for each day's problems; live in vital union with Him (Col. 2:6, *The Living Bible*.).

Lesson 6

Colossians 3:5–4:6

Christianity in Action

Up to this point Paul has written about doctrine: first, true doctrine (1:1–2:3); then, false doctrine (2:4–3:4). Now in the typical Pauline pattern, he directs attention to practical Christian living. Christian living springs from Christian life. The passage of this lesson shows us Christianity in action, in the person of the believer. One example of the many commands and exhortations is "Whatsoever ye do in word or deed, do all in the name of the Lord Jesus, giving thanks to God and the Father by him" (3:17).

I. PREPARATION FOR STUDY

1. Review again the context of this passage, as shown on the following diagram.

CONTEXT OF COLOSSIANS 3:5—4:6

1:1	1:13	2:4	3:5	4:7 4:18
TRUE DOCTRINE		FALSE DOCTRINE	CHRISTIAN LIVING	CHRISTIAN FELLOWSHIP
mainly doctrinal			mainly practical	mainly personal

2. What areas of everyday life would you expect to be covered by a New Testament writer giving counsel on Christian living?

II. ANALYSIS

Segment to be analyzed: 3:5–4:6
Paragraph divisions: at verses 3:5, 12, 18; 4:2

A. General Analysis

1. Read the segment through paragraph by paragraph.
2. Are paragraphs 3:5-11 and 3:12-17 similar in general content?
How do the phrases "put off" (3:8) and "put on" (3:12) suggest a
difference between the paragraphs?

_____

_____

3. What is 3:18–4:1 about?

_____

_____

Why is 4:1 included in this paragraph?

_____

_____

4. As you continue your study of this segment, keep in mind the
following outline:

Christianity in Action
1. In one's personal life (3:5-17)
2. In the Christian home (3:18–4:1)
3. Final exhortations (4:2-6)

B. Paragraph Analysis

1. *Paragraph 3:5-11*
Are the commands of this paragraph mainly positive or negative?

_____

Compare "mortify" and "put off" (3:8).

_____

_____

Compare the command "put off" (3:8) and the declarative statement "ye have put off" (3:9). What is the object in each case?

_____

_____

_____

What is the main contrast between 3:9 and 3:10?

_____

_____

Make a list of the various commands of this paragraph. Study the list carefully.

_____

_____

_____

What is the bright concluding statement of the paragraph? (Recall this as being a key phrase for Survey Chart D.) What is its context?

_____

_____

_____

2. *Paragraph 3:12-17*
Is this paragraph mainly negative or positive? Compare such key words as "put on" (3:12), "rule" (3:15), and "dwell" (3:16).

_____

_____

_____

_____

What references to Christ are made here? How is practical Christian living involved in each case?

_____

_____

_____

Make a list of the exhortations and commands of the paragraph. Compare this list with the one made for the previous paragraph.

_____

_____

_____

_____

Why is attitude so important in a person's life?

_____

_____

What attitudes are urged in these verses?

_____

_____

How is 3:17 a concluding verse for the section 3:5-17?

_____

_____

3. *Paragraph 3:18—4:1*
Record below the six members (or groups) of a Christian household and the commands given to each.

MEMBERS	COMMANDS
①	
②	
③	
④	
⑤	
⑥	

47

To which group does Paul write the most? Can you account for such disproportion?

_____

_____

4. Paragraph 4:2-6
What are the commands of this paragraph?

_____

_____

_____

How does the paragraph serve as a conclusion to the main body of the epistle? (The remainder of the epistle, 4:7-18, mainly records salutations and other personal concluding notes.)

_____

_____

III. NOTES

1. *"Mortify therefore your members which are upon the earth"* (3:5). The "members" are not bodily organs as such but more likely "bodily attitudes and actions as expressive of 'the old man'"[1] (Cf. Rom. 7:23; 8:13). Positionally the believer is already "dead with Christ" (2:20; 3:3). Experientially he should be living each day with the steady determination and will to reflect that position.

2. *"Barbarian, Scythian"* (3:11). In Paul's day non-Greeks were referred to as barbarians. Scythians, an uncivilized people who lived north of the Black Sea, were a type of the lowest class of barbarians.

3. *"Let the peace of God rule in your hearts"* (3:15). The word translated "rule" means literally "to act as an umpire."

4. *"Redeeming the time"* (4:5). This phrase means "buying up the opportunity."

5. *"Speech . . . seasoned with salt"* (4:6). Salt has many uses, including preserving foods and making them pleasant to the taste. Here the illustration refers to the kind of talking that is pleasant and attractive to others, avoiding pointless argument.

1. E. Earle Ellis, "The Epistle to the Colosians," p. 1343.

IV. FOR THOUGHT AND DISCUSSION

1. Think of different ways Christ can be magnified in the lives of His children in the home, with the next-door neighbor, at the office or shop.

2. Note that the ministry of teaching and admonishing is associated with the singing of psalms, hymns, and spiritual songs (3:16). Study the words of one or two hymns in your church hymnal and observe how much doctrine and practical living is taught.

3. How important is thankfulness? What different references to thanksgiving appear in this passage?

4. What parts of this Scripture passage especially blessed you as you studied this lesson?

V. FURTHER STUDY

Study what the New Testament teaches about future rewards and retribution. Begin with Colossians 3:24-25.

VI. WORDS TO PONDER

Be gentle and ready to forgive; never hold grudges. Remember, the Lord forgave you, so you must forgive others (Col. 3:13, *The Living Bible*).

Personal Greetings and Salutations

This concluding passage of Paul's letter to the Colossians is filled with personal greetings and salutations. Bible students often overlook precious gems hidden among lines like these. As you study the twelve verses keep your eyes and heart open to what God has for you here. You will not be disappointed.

I. PREPARATION FOR STUDY

1. Review your studies of the past lessons on Colossians by glancing once again at the survey Chart D. A brief survey of the epistle is shown on Chart I.

BRIEF SURVEY OF COLOSSIANS   **Chart I**

1:1	1:13	2:4	3:5	4:7 4:18
PERSONAL	DOCTRINAL	POLEMICAL	HORTATORY	PERSONAL
INTRODUCTION	TRUE DOCTRINE	FALSE DOCTRINE	CHRISTIAN LIVING	CONCLUSION
	mainly doctrinal		mainly practical	mainly personal

2. Read 4:7-18, and list all the names of persons cited in these closing lines. Then learn as much as you can about each person from a Bible dictionary or an exhaustive concordance. This is your personal introduction to Paul's friends.

II. ANALYSIS

Segment to be analyzed: 4:7-18
Paragraph divisions: at verses 4:7, 10, 15, 18

Scan the entire segment to see why new paragraphs are made at the divisions shown above. Compare your observations with the outline shown on the left-hand side of Chart J. Are all of the persons mentioned in the passage believers?

Observe on the chart that the first three names mentioned in the second paragraph are Jewish names and the second three are Gentile names.

Use Chart J as a worksheet to record your observations. The two primary things to look for are (1) how each person is identified and (2) what services Paul's friends were rendering in the cause of the gospel.

III. NOTES

1. *"That he might know your estate"* (4:8). The better-attested reading is "that ye might know our estate." Compare the readings of various versions. Also, compare Ephesians 6:21.

2. *"Aristarchus my fellow prisoner"* (4:10). This friend of Paul may have voluntarily shared Paul's imprisonment so that he could be with him.

3. *"Marcus, sister's son to Barnabas"* (4:10). The translation should be, "Marcus, cousin of Barnabas" (see Berkeley). This was John Mark, author of the second gospel, who with Barnabas accompanied Paul on his first missionary journey. This is the first mention of him by Paul since the rupture of Acts 15:39, fourteen years earlier.

4. *"The church which is in his house"* (4:15). Such house-churches were common in the infant years of the Christian church, when new local groups of believers had no building in which to worship. (Cf. Acts 12:12; Rom. 16:5; 1 Cor. 16:19; Philem. 2.) There is no evidence of church building by Christian groups before the third century.

5. *"Epistle from Laodicea"* (4:16). Nothing certain is known of this letter. Some think it is a reference to Paul's letter to the Ephesians or to Philemon.

OUTLINE		NAME	HOW IDENTIFIED	MINISTRY
PAUL'S MESSENGERS		4:7 TYCHICUS		
		ONESIMUS		
GREETINGS FROM THESE	JEWISH CHRISTIANS	4:10 ARISTARCHUS		
		MARCUS		
		JUSTUS		
	GENTILE CHRISTIANS	EPAPHRAS		
		LUKE		
		DEMAS		
GREETINGS TO THESE		4:15 NYMPHAS		
		ARCHIPPUS		
		4:18 PAUL		

6. *"The salutation by the hand of me Paul"* (4:18). The epistle itself was dictated by Paul to a scribe, with Paul writing this last line himself to authenticate the letter's origin.

IV. FOR THOUGHT AND DISCUSSION

Derive as many practical lessons from this passage as you can. Consider the following:

1. What is suggested by each of these: fellow servant (4:7); fellow prisoner (4:10); fellow worker (4:11).
2. Note that no description or commendation is given in connection with Demas (4:14). May this be a foreshadowing of the tragic note of 2 Timothy 4:10, written six years later?
3. In verses 7-14, what words and phrases does Paul use to describe Christians?
4. Why did Paul urge ministers like Archippus to "take heed" to their ministry? (Cf.2 Tim. 1: 6.) What were the pitfalls endangering a minister of the gospel? What are the dangers today?

V. FURTHER STUDY

Develop in more detail a character study of each of the persons mentioned in this concluding passage of Colossians.

A CONCLUDING NOTE

Paul's farewell salutation (4:18) is brief but moving. The two key words are *hand* and *bonds*. What do you think went through the apostle's mind as he signed the letter, possibly even to the sound of clanging chains as he moved his hand to write? Whatever were those thoughts, the apostle kept on triumphing in the truth of the gospel of Christ. Truly, "the sound of pen and chains together is [a] sign that the preacher's chains cannot bind the word of God."[1] Paul had no doubt that his letter to the saints living in the Lycus Valley would bring forth eternal fruit to the glory of Christ, who "is all and in all." "Grace be with you," he wrote. And then, "Amen."

---

1. J. Ithel Jones, "The Epistle to the Colossians," p. 1051.

Lesson 8
Paul's Letter to Philemon

Philemon is the shortest of Paul's writings, a masterpiece of grace-ful, tactful, and delicate pleading for a forgiving spirit. Forgive-ness is the letter's main message, made a part of the Scriptures by the inspiration of the Holy Spirit.

This personal correspondence of Paul has been described as "a model letter written by a master of letter writing." If you agree that there is a vital Christian ministry in the writing of letters, de-termine now to learn from this epistle some practical lessons on how to make your own letters effective for Christ.

I. PREPARATION FOR STUDY

A. Background of the Letter

1. *Names in the Letter*
    (a) Philemon was a well-to-do Christian friend of Paul, living in or near Colosse. He was probably the husband of Apphia and father of Archippus, two persons named in Philemon 2. The name Philemon means *loving*.
    (b) Onesimus was a household servant of Philemon, who probably came to know Paul intimately after his conversion at Rome. His name means *useful*, or *profitable*, a common nickname for slaves.
    (c) The names cited in Philemon 23-24 were studied in Les-son 7 in connection with the Colossian epistle.

2. *Occasion of the Letter*
Onesimus had apparently stolen money or goods from his master, Philemon (Philem. 18) and fled to Rome like so many other runaway slaves. Through circumstances unknown to us he came

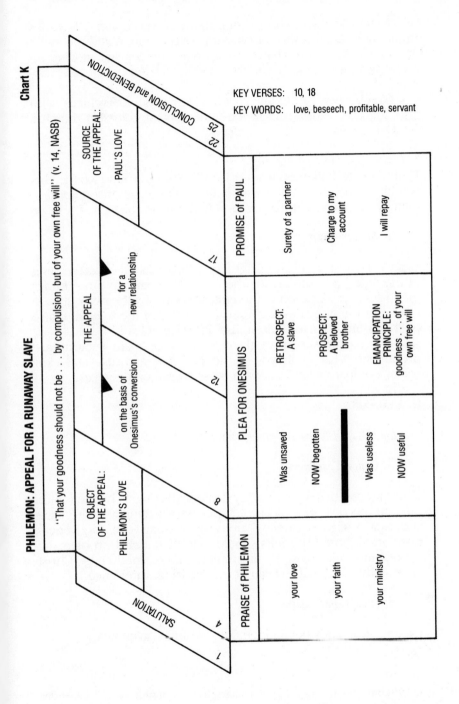

Chart K

PHILEMON: APPEAL FOR A RUNAWAY SLAVE

"That your goodness should not be . . . by compulsion, but of your own free will" (v. 14, NASB)

KEY VERSES: 10, 18

KEY WORDS: love, beseech, profitable, servant

SALUTATION — 1–4

OBJECT OF THE APPEAL: PHILEMON'S LOVE

THE APPEAL
- on the basis of Onesimus's conversion — 8–12
- for a new relationship — 12–17

SOURCE OF THE APPEAL: PAUL'S LOVE — 17–22

CONCLUSION and BENEDICTION — 22–25

PRAISE of PHILEMON
- your love
- your faith
- your ministry

PLEA FOR ONESIMUS
- Was unsaved / NOW begotten
- Was useless / NOW useful
- RETROSPECT: A slave
- PROSPECT: A beloved brother
- EMANCIPATION PRINCIPLE: goodness . . . of your own free will

PROMISE of PAUL
- Surety of a partner
- Charge to my account
- I will repay

in contact with Paul, who led him to the Lord (Philem. 10). Paul's immediate concern was for Onesimus's restoration and reconciliation with Philemon. Hence the apostle's tender and moving intercessory letter to his close friend Philemon on behalf of Onesimus.

The bearers of the letter were Onesimus and Tychicus, who also delivered Paul's letter to the Ephesian and Colossian churches (cf. Col. 4:7-9).

3. Place and Date of Writing
Paul wrote to Philemon from prison in Rome, around A.D.61. This was about the same time he wrote the other three prison epistles, namely Colossians, Ephesians, and Philippians. (See Chart A.)

B. Survey Chart

Chart K is a survey of this brief letter. First make a casual reading of the letter, and then study the chart. Note among other things the orderly progression of thought, as shown by the two outlines: Object of the Appeal—The Appeal—Source of the Appeal; Praise of Philemon—Plea for Onesimus—Promise of Paul.

From your survey of the epistle, what main subjects are prominent? What would you consider to be key words—and a key verse? Compare your ideas with those shown on the chart.

II. ANALYSIS

Paragraph divisions: at verses 1, 4, 8, 12, 17, 22[1]

A. General Analysis

There are various ways to study this epistle. One is by the topical method. Record on a piece of paper what is taught in the letter about each of the following subjects: Christian love, forgiveness, restoration, how Christians should deal with a civil problem, accountability, intercession, illustration of redemption by Christ. (The study of this subject can be an inspiring experience.)

B. Paragraph Analysis

Expand your study beyond the few questions given below.

---

1. Most Bible versions begin a new paragraph at v. 21 instead of v. 22. Either division can be justified.

1. *Paragraph vv. 1-3*
In what different ways are Christians identified in this salutation?
2. *Paragraph vv. 4-7*
What is taught here about faith and love?
3. *Paragraph vv. 8-11*
Where does the name Onesimus appear? Is this the first occurrence in the letter? Do you see any tact on Paul's part in delaying this specific reference in his letter? Read verses 10 and 11 together, translating the name Onesimus by its literal meaning, profitable. What is Paul's method here? Do you think Paul had a special reason for mentioning his imprisonment (v. 9) and bonds (v. 10) at this point?
4. *Paragraph vv. 12-16*
Note the repeated appeal "receive him." (The phrase is repeated again in v. 17.) What does Paul say about this in each case?
What is the impact of the phrase "not . . . of necessity, but willingly" (v 14)?
5. *Paragraph vv. 17-21*
What is Paul's method of persuasion in these verses? Observe how Paul involves himself in Onesimus's plight. Reflect on the significance of each of these phrases:
"receive him as myself" (v 17). "put that on mine account" (v. 18);
"I will repay it" (v. 19); "thou owest unto me" (v. 19).
Apply the above phrases, by way of illustration, to the substitutionary work of Christ for the sinner.
6. *Paragraph vv. 22-25*
What truths about Christian fellowship do you learn from these concluding verses of the epistle?

III. NOTES

1. *"Paul the aged"* (v 9). Paul was about sixty years old and prematurely aged from persecutions and other hardships in the ministry when he wrote this letter. Some ancient manuscripts read "the ambassador" instead of "the aged," but, as one writer comments, the latter is "the better attested reading and more appropriate in the context."[2]
2. *"A servant"* (v. 16). The Greek is *doulos,* which may be translated by the stronger word "bond servant."
3. *"If he hath wronged thee"* (v. 18). Under Roman law, fugitive slaves were liable to severest punishment. For example, "recovered slaves were branded on the forehead, condemned to

2. T. E. Robertson, "The Epistle to Philemon," in *The New Bible Commentary*, p. 1086.

double labor, and sometimes thrown to the beasts in the amphitheatre."[3]

4. *"Knowing that thou wilt also do more than I say"* (v. 21). Some think that this was a hint to release Onesimus from his servitude.

IV. FOR THOUGHT AND DISCUSSION

1. It has been said that the real character of a man is learned more accurately from his private letters than from his public correspondence. What does the letter to Philemon tell you about Paul?

2. What examples of tact and wisdom do you see in the letter? For example, observe that Paul does not use such words as *stole* or *fled* when referring to Onesimus.

3. What does this epistle teach about the master-servant relationship, when both are Christians? Compare Colossians 3:22–4:1. Extend this application to related situations today, such as that of employer-employee.

4. Ponder the transformation: "in time past . . . unprofitable, but now profitable" (v. 11). Alexander Maclaren comments on this, "Christianity knows nothing of hopeless cases. It professes its ability to take the most crooked stick and bring it straight, to flash a new power into the blackest carbon, which will turn it into a diamond."[4]

V. FURTHER STUDY

Much has been written about the subject of slavery, including what the New Testament says about it. It has been observed, for example, that Paul does not make a frontal attack in his letter to Philemon upon the institution of slavery, which was widespread throughout the Roman empire. Rather he sets forth principles and patterns of Christian conduct and relationships that inevitably must bring about the destruction of the institution, when consistently applied. Study this subject further, using the New Testament and outside helps for your sources.

3. Marvin R. Vincent, *Word Studies in the New Testament*, 3:519.
4. Quoted by Marvin R. Vincent, *Word Studies in the New Testament*, 3:520.

CONCLUDING THOUGHTS

"For love's sake I . . . beseech thee . . . for . . . Onesimus" (Philem. 9-10).
Christian love has time for people, whoever they are and whatever their needs.

> Even as Christ did for us with God the Father, thus also doth St. Paul for Onesimus with Philemon; for Christ also stripped Himself of His right, and by love and humility enforced the Father to lay aside His wrath and power, and to take us to His grace for the sake of Christ, Who lovingly pleadeth our cause, and with all His heart layeth Himself out for us.[5]

The Christ who inspired Paul to plead for Onesimus was the same Christ of Paul's letters to the Ephesians: "In Him we have redemption through His blood"; to the Philippians: "To me to live is Christ"; and to the Colossians: "Christ is all, and in all." May you in your Bible studies return often to these prison epistles, to be refreshed and revived anew as you fellowship with Jesus your Lord.

5. Martin Luther, quoted in W. Graham Scroggie, *Know Your Bible*, 2:201-2.

Bibliography

COMMENTARIES AND TOPICAL STUDIES

Bruce, F. F. *The Epistles to the Colossians,* Philemon and Ephesians, Grand Rapids: Eerdmans, 1984,

Ellis, E. Earle. "The Epistle to the Colossians." In *The Wycliffe Bible Commentary,* edited by Charles F. Pfeiffer and Everett F. Harrison. Chicago: Moody, 1962.

Hendricksen, William. *Exposition of Colossians and Philemon.* Grand Rapids: Baker, 1964.

Jones, J. Ithel. "The Epistle to the Colossians." In *The New Bible* Commentary, edited by F. Davidson. Grand Rapids: Eerdmans, 1953.

Lenski, R. C. H. *The Interpretation of St. Paul's Epistles to the Colossians, to the Thessalonians, to Timothy, to Titus and to Philemon.* Columbus: Wartburg, 1937.

Moule, C. F. D. *The Epistles to Colossians and Philemon.* Cambridge: U. Press, 1958.

Rees, Paul S. *The Epistles to the Philippians, Colossians, and Philemon,* Grand Rapids: Baker, 1964.

Robertson, T. E. "The Epistle to Philemon." In *The New Bible Commentary,* edited by F. Davidson. Grand Rapids: Eerdmans, 1953.

Scroggie, W. Graham. *Know Your Bible.* Vol. 2. London: Pickering & Inglis, n.d.

Simpson, E. K., and Bruce, F. F. *Commentary on the Epistles to the Ephesians and the Colossians.* Grand Rapids: Eerdmans, 1957.

Thomas, William. *Studies in Colossians and Philemon.* Grand Rapids: Kregel, 1986.

Wuest, Kenneth S. *Ephesians and Colossians in the Greek New Testament.* Grand Rapids: Eerdmans, 1954.

RESOURCES FOR FURTHER STUDY

Baxter, J. Sidlow. *Explore the Book.* Grand Rapids: Zondervan, 1960.

Bruce, F. F. *The Letters of Paul: Expanded Paraphrase.* Grand Rapids: Eerdmans, 1965.

Everyday Bible. New Testament Study Edition. Minneapolis: World Wide, 1988.

Hiebert, D. Edmond. *An Introduction to the Pauline Epistles.* Chicago: Moody, 1954.

Jensen, Irving L. *Jensen's Survey of the New Testament.* Chicago: Moody, 1981.

Nave, Orville J. *Nave's Topical Bible.* Chicago: Moody, n.d.

New International Version Study Bible. Grand Rapids: Zondervan, 1985.

Phillips, John. *Exploring the Scriptures.* Chicago: Moody, 1965.

Ryrie Study Bible. Chicago: Moody, 1985.

Strong, James. *The Exhaustive Concordance of the Bible.* New York: Abingdon, 1890.

Tenney, Merrill C., ed. *The Zondervan Pictorial Bible Dictionary.* Grand Rapids: Zondervan, 1963.

Unger, Merrill F. *The New Unger's Bible Handbook.* Chicago: Moody, 1984.

_____. *New Unger's Bible Dictionary.* Chicago: Moody, 1988.

Vincent, Marvin R. *Word Studies in the New Testament.* Grand Rapids: Eerdmans, 1946.

Vine, W. E. *An Expository Dictionary of New Testament Words.* Westwood.